In the Grip of Grace

poems by

Marianne Mersereau

Finishing Line Press
Georgetown, Kentucky

In the Grip of Grace

Copyright © 2024 by Marianne Mersereau
ISBN 979-8-88838-561-6 First Edition
All rights reserved under International and Pan-American Copyright Conventions. No part of this book may be reproduced in any manner whatsoever without written permission from the publisher, except in the case of brief quotations embodied in critical articles and reviews.

Publisher: Leah Huete de Maines
Editor: Christen Kincaid
Cover Art: Marcia Terry
Author Photo: Jean Kercheval
Cover Design: Elizabeth Maines McCleavy

Order online: www.finishinglinepress.com
also available on amazon.com

Author inquiries and mail orders:
Finishing Line Press
PO Box 1626
Georgetown, Kentucky 40324
USA

Contents

Sleeping with the Serpent 1
Why I Eat Pears on My Birthday 2
Bee Whispering 3
Grapevines 4
Groundhog Day 5
Elephants Remembered 6
Storytellers 7
Blood Verse 8
Keeping the Peace 9
Miracle in the Chicken Coop Chapel 10
The Visitation 11
Sonnet for the Pit Ponies 12
Bats in the Chimney 13
Cedar Hill 14
What You Can Do Will Surprise You 15
Skirted Soldiers 16
On Becoming a Writer 17
War Ghosts in the Attic 18
Blue Ridges 19
Civil War Souvenirs 20
He Was Most Afraid of Lightning 21
Elegy for My Uncle's Kidney 22
Early Frost 23
Pearl Harbor 24
I'm Told How to Get a Pretty Man 25
Marry Up 26
Barn Swing 27
Dominion Over All 28

Pocket Knife 29

Bees and Tobacco 30

Buzzard's Roost 31

A Bundle of Gladioli 32

Ode to My First Grade Teacher 33

Learning to Whistle...34

Smashing Satan in the Seventies..36

Appalachian Goddess 37

Irish Roots 38

Grave Finder 39

Day Flowers 40

At Twilight...41

Winter Births 42

Hoeing in the Drought 43

Umbilical Cord 44

In Which My Parents Are Resurrected..45

Scattering the Locks 48

"And yet they, who are long gone, are in us, as predisposition, as burden upon our destiny." ~Rainer Maria Rilke

~

"The necessity to remember the past is what the poem is much more about than the actual incident." ~Natasha Trethewey

Sleeping with the Serpent

~For Aunt Mary Ellen

On threshing day, she said,
we emptied the straw tick mattresses
poured the old chaff into the pig sty,
washed the cotton sacks and hung them
to dry in early autumn sun.

None of us saw the black snake slither
into the pile of new straw.
He did not move when we picked up the stack
and stuffed it into the large pillow case,
sewing the prison shut.

Uncle slept atop the hibernating serpent
until spring came, the mattresses were
once again emptied for washing, and out
crawled the survivor—
well rested, resurrected.

Why I Eat Pears on My Birthday

It all began in the birthing room
in the house where I was born—
the front bedroom with its hardwood floors
fireplace, wallpaper, lace curtains
and view of the old pear tree in the yard
where ripe yellow fruit of late summer
dropped and all my mother wanted
after I was born was someone to bring
her a perfect pear from that tree.

In the softening light of September,
I slice a wide-hipped mother shaped pear
in half on my birthday, close my eyes
and remember the room in which I took
my first breath, my mother's labor,
the window raised, curtains blowing-
and outside, the pear tree loaded.
I honor her by taking this one sweet life
and squeezing all the juice I can from it.

Bee Whispering

When my beekeeper Grandpa passed away, no one
remembered the ancient Celtic custom of telling his bees.

In the days following his death, Grandma complained of ghosts
whispering in her ears at night and a strange buzzing noise.

When she arrived at the hive to assume his duties,
she found it empty and the whole colony attached to an oak limb.

Unlike a swarm, this is an abscond, when the bees decide they've
had enough, clean, pack up and leave with the queen.

Grandma apologized to the bees, captured the cluster in a sack
returned them to the old hive, kept the queen caged underneath

fed her sugar syrup until the workers rebuilt the comb, she
was released, the whispering ceased, and Grandpa rested in peace.

Grapevines

She planted them to climb every structure on the farm,
they crawled across the barn, the chicken coop and house,
letting my mother and aunts open the bedroom
window, reach out and pluck the purple fruit.

Great grandmother made her wine during prohibition,
gave my ten-year-old mother sips of the rich merlot
in the cellar surrounded by the scent of harvested potatoes
and apples mingled with oak, rows of canned green

beans, corn, and jelly lining the shelves
and grandmother's laughter rising up from the
darkness. Everyone said she was crazy
but turns out she was just tipsy.

The more she drank, the more she talked of half-siblings,
unwed mothers, flying saucers, Big Foot sightings,
and whatever she said in the cellar stayed there
fermenting with the forbidden juice.

Groundhog Day

The rodent poked his head out of the hole
and my granddaddy shot him with his rifle

because he needed that groundhog's hide
for his new banjo head.

He admired the tough-skinned animal
but didn't like the holes it dug in the orchard

He carved curly maple, walnut and poplar
to make the banjo's bridge, tailpiece

fingerboard and nut. Grandma hated his playing
when he drank too much whiskey

and played what she called Devils Music:
Going up Cripple Creek and *Little Brown Jug*

Had he played *Amazing Grace* instead, I wonder
if that sweet sound might have saved her

from hearing the groundhog's cry in every note,
erasing the shadows from the sounds.

Elephants Remembered

My mother saw elephants, not in a zoo or circus,
but on Virginia's Wilderness Road.

Trainers marched them up steep slopes
past tobacco barns, grain silos and country stores.

They lumbered toward the big tent in Tennessee
in 1939, and I believe they remembered

Mary, their beloved ancestor hung from a crane
in Erwin, 1916. She moved out of the parade line

to get a tasty piece of watermelon and the trainer
hit her with a whip. Her abscessed teeth made her cranky,

causing her to kill him in rage. *Crucify her*, the crowd
shouted, and they buried her in the rail yard

thinking she'd be forgotten, forgetting how loud bones speak.

Storytellers

Restless spirits of the dead
roamed the ridges,
made their way into stories
my kinfolk told.

Mama called these ghosts, haints,
shared how they gathered
at the foot of her bed
pulled the covers and taunted her.

Uncle described
hearing a dog behind him,
turned to see it disappeared,
my aunt floating in strange light.

Once a friend complained to me
of a ghost knocking books
from her nightstand and wandering
through her house.

His name is Will, I told her
and she was shocked knowing
she'd never talked to me
about Will who died
in a drowning accident
only four months prior,

and I'd never heard from
departed souls who have stories
of their own.

Blood Verse

Ezekiel 16:6

Like a secret formula or recipe
handed down through the generations
my grandmother first told me the story

how my brother fell and cut his head on a rock
and the bleeding would not stop
until my great-grandmother recited the verse three times
and spoke my brother's full name

It works with animals too, she said
for horses hemorrhaging after giving birth or
cows after their horns are removed—
You just speak the words and the blood stops.

Keeping the Peace

Every Sunday, my great grandfather
walked a mile to the small country church
carrying his old tattered Bible
but he never ventured inside.

Leaning against the hickory tree
he listened to the hymns and sermon,
hounds praying across the hill
and crows singing overhead.

He left at the last amen and walked home
alone. No one rushed out to ask for
a donation, shake his hand or wish him
a good day. He kept his peace to himself.

Miracle in the Chicken Coop Chapel

"With God, all things are possible."
~Jesus (Matthew 19:26)

I'm sure many miracles
took place in the chickens' home-
like the narrow escape from a fox or snake,
but the one that stands out
is the tongue that was reattached.

My aunt tells the story this way:
How her sister fell and sliced her tongue
almost completely off. My grandmother
picked her up and ran into the chicken coop,

praying in the name
of the Father, the Son, and the Holy Ghost
as the hens squawked their
praise in that sacred space. The torn
tongue was made whole again.

When you live far from the doctors
and you don't have a car nor money to pay them,
you learn to believe in impossibilities.

The Visitation

~For Aunt Rosie

The mantel, like an altar, held all the
sacred items, knickknacks of importance:
a small box of cards with Bible verses, a tiny
six pack of miniature coke bottles, and in
the center, a photo of Henrich Hofmann's
painting of Christ at 33.

As a child, my aunt had this image of Christ fixed
in her mind, so she recognized him one day
when he floated in through a window and stood
beside her and her younger brother, placing
one hand on each of them. After a while
he went back out the window into the sky.

She's told this story many times over the years
and holds fast to the facts at age eighty without
witnesses. Her mother had gone to the spring
to fetch water and left her alone with her brother.
I place a magnet of the Christ image on the altar
of my refrigerator, stare at it and wonder:

Might Jesus show up one day when I'm standing
alone at the kitchen sink or putting a casserole
into the oven, or am I too old for this kind of vision?

Sonnet for the Pit Ponies

Gus, Rufus, Charlie and Pip, left to starve
on the blasted tops of the blue ridges
after spending most of your lives underground,
you were hand fed, never learned to crop grass.

You pulled the coal cars to the surface, a sort of
phoenix in fur and hooves, a hard working
co-worker. Where was the miracle in the
machines that followed? You were loved

by miners like my uncle who fed you from
his lunch pail—half a sandwich, a piece of cake
or apple core, and offered to give you a home
but the company turned him down and

you spent your retirement years like he did,
struggling to breathe with dust covered lungs.

Bats in the Chimney

Of all the places they could have
chosen to roost, why did they
pick our chimney? Flying into
the living room inflicting fear
of rabies. My father felt

he had no choice but to kill them
with pesticides. Some years later,
we scratched mosquito bites
as he told me he regretted killing
the bats, is haunted by

the memory of their small bodies
lying on the fireplace grate, and I
think of them as I look at the
container of non-organic blueberries
with its warning to rinse before eating

read about wild cats dying slow
deaths after eating poisoned rats.

Cedar Hill

Once
cleared for the
cows to graze, when they
moved on, the trees came back
some scrappy, others perfect Christmas
triangles. My brother cut one for our living
room window where it braved the annual rituals.
In the fifties, my father sold enough to pay that year's
taxes. With time, everyone lost interest in cedars. Now they
stand on the hill unbothered by humans
like a silent green-robed choir before
an audience of one.

What You Can Do Will Surprise You

My mother assures me of this
her story as proof.

Raised on less than a dime
in a house with no indoor plumbing,

her father died when she was nineteen,
his neck broken in a car wreck.

She never talked about him much,
just did what she had to do:

joined the Women's Army Corps,
served as a post-WWII nurse.

Of the wounded soldiers she said,
They just kept coming.

I surprised myself a few times
doing what I had to do:

eating peanut butter sandwiches
for a week waiting for my paycheck

giving birth without an epidural
because it was too late to get one.

I trace the letter M on my palm:
Letting her go was hardest.

Skirted Soldiers

My mother and aunts wore
olive-drab jackets
with gold tone buttons
the color of Montana mornings
the kind that make
horses test their fences.

In their knee length skirts
they took care not to walk
up the stairs while male
soldiers stood at the bottom
cat calling, whistling, asking
Who wants to get pregnant?

Army Corps women ignored
lunging kisses, endured
smear campaigns claiming
they were of low morality
and persisted in their service
without laws to assist them.

Colonel Oveta Hobby
led them to victory in the 50's
as they achieved ranks
of Corporal and Sergeant,
changed the world
with a skirted twirl.

On Becoming a Writer

At 14, my uncle lied about his age
to enlist in the army, his ticket
off the Virginia farm, out of the holler.

On a ship in San Francisco, he
faked shaving till his real age
became known and he was sent home.

At 18, he grew a beard, re-enlisted
and went to Korea where he
never wrote letters to anyone.

My grandmother was left to worry,
wonder and pray till one day he
reappeared physically unharmed.

When he approached eighty,
he scribbled a note to me
on a Christmas card:

I've never been much of a writer,
but I'm doing fine,
still fighting on.

I clutch the card, marvel at the shaky
handwriting of a survivor, one who
had finally become a writer.

War Ghosts in the Attic

We grew up hearing the story
of the wooden legs
and how they used to be in the attic
of our old farmhouse
and got up to walk around at night.

They belonged to the former owner,
a Veteran of WWI who lost his real legs
on a battlefield in France.

My father tried to convince my mother
that the attic sounds were mice,
but they haunted her, so he burned them
in a bonfire and the attic became quiet

but the ghosts from my father's past
kept walking through his dreams,
crying out in his sleep, reminding him
of how he'd lost pieces of his right leg
on a battlefield in WWII.

Blue Ridges

The hills my father roamed in his life
were similar—rugged slopes rising
above lush valleys, and I wish to see them
before their scars—Wallens Ridge before
Daniel Boone, General Lee and Massey Coal,
Okinawa's Kakazu before kamikazes,
banzais and suicide cliff dives.

I picture him as a child climbing
in Tennessee gathering holly for Christmas,
hunting squirrel and deer with his shotgun,
and years later crossing Conical Hill
carrying a fallen comrade, and a different
kind of weapon. I study the witnesses
on these ridges: palm, cherry, dogwood, cedar.

Civil War Souvenirs

Each spring,
with click of hoe
or blade of plow,
while weeding the bean patch
or planting tobacco,
we got some more
reminders of that war:
One year a quarter-sized circle
from a Union horse bridle,
the next a metal buckle
with a Confederate cross.
We hung them in the shed,
marveled at how the sod
refused to let us forget
how much was lost
and gained from all that pain.

He Was Most Afraid of Lightning

Not of tumbling on the tractor
getting bitten by a copperhead
running out of money
having no health or crop insurance
losing the tobacco plants
to cut worms,
black shank disease or drought.

No, my father feared the dark clouds
electric air, flattened fields
cows sheltering underneath trees
the sudden jagged flash
of red orange yellow missile
searching the ground
for the tallest target.

We sat once on the porch
watching a storm,
saw a lone hay bale on a distant field
become a torch and my brother
recalled the terror
of being struck
while riding his bike,
stunned that
he was alive to tell us about it.

Elegy for My Uncle's Kidney

> *"Two are better than one for they have a better return for their labor."*
> *~Ecclesiastes 4:9*

All I knew of the war in Viet Nam
is that my mom's little brother
was lucky not to have died there.

He lost one of his kidneys, the bean-
shaped twin comrades that work
together to cleanse the blood twice a day.

When one is gone, the other carries on,
the labor greater, the return always
a reminder of the loss.

Early Frost

You told me the story
as if entrusting me
with silver I'd keep safe
long after you left.

It was the year of the early frost
covering the tobacco crop,
your worst memory you said
and I was surprised.

I thought surely it would
have been the moment
you stepped onto that
land mine in Saipan,

not the September morning
you awoke to your father
in the hospital, no neighbors
coming to your aid

leaves bitten, your daddy dying,
and not a thing you could do.

Pearl Harbor

Just another sunny day
like December 7, 1941
was just another day.

Aloha, Daddy,

I speak into the cell phone.
He's eighty-four and far away.

I try to imagine him here
after the bombing,

his ship leaving for Okinawa.
He tells me that was a long time ago.

You want a souvenir, perhaps a cap?

His souvenir is the scar on his leg,
seared into memory.

Forty days in the hospital
like Jesus in the desert.

As kids, we knew which side of his lap
could not hold us.

I buy him a cap that he wears with pride,
try to feel his footprints on Waikiki-

Give thanks his name is not on the memorial.

I'm Told How to Get a Pretty Man

You want to get a
pretty man someday? Then
you gotta learn to make a pretty
bed, my granny said. Wash the sheets
in spring water, hang them
outside to dry so sunshine
can seep into their seams,
make them smell
like pure love. Lay a fancy
quilt on top of the sheets—one with
a romantic pattern like
Double Wedding Ring. Make
sure the tiny stitches are
strong enough to
hold you and your pretty
man together forever.

Marry Up

~For My Maternal Grandmother

We are on the back porch of her small house
pulling clothes through the ringer washing machine
talking about my future
My advice is to marry up, she says
in her deep mountain accent,
speaks local family names she considers down
and some that are up, sorting them like laundry.
We carry the basket of wet clothes into the yard.
She reaches down, picks up a towel
and hangs it on the line, while in my head,
I invent names she's never heard.

Barn Swing

We strung hay
bale twine from the barn rafters
and fashioned a seat for our swing from an old
empty bag of fertilizer. Pumping our legs hard, we came
eye to eye with the tiny sleeping owl, swallow nests and a million
spider webs, met the scent of dried manure, hay,
tobacco and tractor grease, learned to
count how many lifts the string
would allow and how to fall
so we could get back up
and do it again. Years later
we shuffled through embers
after the fire nothing
but memories
to swing us
forward.

Dominion Over All

Thunder shook our windows. Wind
moved the barn two inches, and then
there was the ball of fire big
as a tractor tire that
came rolling through
the living room
into the kitchen
struck the refrigerator
dissolved and
knocked out the electricity.

We sat stunned huddled
on the couch, staring
at the fire ball's path
wondering
what if one of us had
walked to the refrigerator,
been standing in
the middle of the room?

Pocket Knife

I am a child of eight
playing outside all day
among the insects:
praying mantis, butterflies,
grasshoppers
leeches in the creek
lightning bugs and a tick
sinking into my scalp.

Daddy sees this dark parasite
in my sun-bleached hair,
pulls from his overall pocket
the Barlow knife
with two blades.
It has cut hay bale twine
whittled poplar sticks
plucked dandelions
and the flowering tops of Burley tobacco.

With the sharp tip, he cuts the tick from my head
and I don't feel a thing
as I watch him drown the pest
in a pool of rubbing alcohol,
wiping the knife blade clean again.

Bees and Tobacco

We see the small cubes on stands
and they appear to us
as miniature stoves, refrigerators, sinks.
We pretend they are toys
and approach to play house.
Opening the door, angry bees fly out.
Like hot grease
they sting our skin
and we run screaming down to the field
where daddy hoes corn
while chewing King Edward tobacco.
He pulls a wad from his mouth,
and puts it on the stings:
the mix of saliva and nicotine
heals all our pain as the bees
return to their kitchen in victory.

Buzzard's Roost

In late summer light we hike
high above the tree line
in land of long, slow vowels and blue ridges,
past cow pies and horse flies.

Then we see them:
vultures roosting on limestone boulders-
timeless as we are.

Their forefathers and ours
once hunted bison in the valley below.

The bison are gone now,
mountain tops removed and
the old homestead an abandoned coalmine.

We peer down with the winged witnesses,
all of us surviving on what's left over.

A Bundle of Gladioli

"I must have flowers, always, and always."
~Claude Monet

Standing on the platform by his seat
I rode with my dad on the red Ford tractor
down our gravel driveway onto the paved road
toward a farm by the river

where a widow grew acres of flowers
among vegetables, tall deep red, magenta,
orange, yellow, violet and purple gladioli.
She cut a large bundle and handed it to me

so thick I could hardly embrace it,
the stalks almost as tall as me
the colors painted on my memory making
that the moment I knew I could not live

without flowers. It was the moment
Monet's obsession became mine, the moment
I understood why he'd sometimes slash
and kick his paintings in frustration

angry at his failed attempts to paint water
lilies and iris exactly as he wished, how he
raged against old age, bad weather and poor
eye sight. How deeply he loved this Earth garden.

Ode to My First Grade Teacher

"A word after a word after a word is power."
~Margaret Atwood

She peers over my shoulder
still, though she's been gone for years
she was also my mother's First Grade
teacher.

Like a guardian angel, a director
from afar, she moves my pencil
across the page, my fingers on the
keyboard.

I wonder if she'd recognize me now
no longer a shy child, my words piled up
like a library, my power like a
poet.

Learning to Whistle

> *"Girls just want to have fun."*
> *~Song Title by Cindi Lauper*

The sound first came out
while I was perched
on the driver's seat of the
Massey Ferguson tractor
parked in the machine shed.

The shed smelled of engine
grease, gasoline, soil,
dried plants and hay, had
three walls and a dirt floor,
hay baler and second tractor.

One wall was covered with
rusty, antique tools, another
decorated with barn swallow
nests and the abandoned
skin of a large black rat snake.

How determined to sit among these
delights pretending to drive
and practice my whistling,
something I'd been working
on for weeks.

Lips puckered, blowing
air through them, waiting for
the sound to emerge. When
finally I figured it out, with
pride, I ran to entertain granny

with this newly acquired skill.
She listened to me and frowned.
A whistling maid and a crowing hen
always come to a very bad end,
she said, It ain't lady-like to whistle.
Not Lady-Like, a phrase I'd heard

before when I laughed too loud,
pretended to smoke or chewed gum
as if it were tobacco, spitting
like I'd seen the men do.

I tried to imagine
my very bad end:
Would I be struck by lightning,
my lips permanently puckered,
or might I end up in hell?

Well, hell or no hell and lady-like
ambitions aside, when all was said and
done, this girl decided all she wanted
was to have some fun.

Smashing Satan in the Seventies

My zealous friend invited me
to help her destroy records
she deemed had the Devil in them
and I agreed.

We took a hammer and smashed
ACDC's Dirty Deeds Done Dirt Cheap,
Alice Cooper and Led Zeppelin
Everything she owned that was not gospel

got destroyed, all of our teenage angst
and hatred of evil hammered out
in rage unleashed on the innocent vinyl,
us standing victorious over Satan in our

long denim skirts, long blonde hair
and King James Bibles, proud and pure.
I didn't know that some years later,
with cropped hair and mini-skirt,

I'd be dancing to those same songs.

Appalachian Goddess

I opened my mouth
sunk my teeth into names
twisted them round on
my tongue: Brilliant Hillbilly
Ignorant Beach Bum
I forgot all I knew
except where I came from:
holler, gap, ridge or hill
A holy roller drinking
from a moonshine still.
I spoke in tongues
I did not understand
Picked up two serpents
with my right hand
Lost my religion
Found my faith
Now I'm a goddess
in the grip of grace.

Irish Roots

I don't know the ancestor's names
but I feel them in my bones.
I bleed green blood,
recall an ancient image
of daffodils dancing
on a hillside
to the sound of fiddles
and clog dancers
on a wooden floor.
I follow a cord from
Appalachian hollows
to a Dublin pub.
My luck runs deep
as peat bogs
buried coal, graveyards
with screaming banshees
and spirits rising to form
a rainbow over my family tree.

Grave Finder

It was what she wanted to do,
we always went in summer

even though winter would've been better
no snakes to dodge, every rock pile a dread.

But the kids were out of school,
so we took my mother in search

of her dead Appalachian ancestors,
down dusty dirt roads through corn fields

past old farm houses, battered barns
and barbed wire fences

searching for sleeping bones
asking strangers

*Mind if we poke around in the graveyard
up yonder on the hill?*

Mama found graves only marked by rocks,
overgrown by kudzu and morning glory.

She was the last person living
to know the place of these dead.

Day Flowers

I'm glad I asked your favorite
flower and song before
the day that you were gone. Your answers
were the simplest: Jesus Loves
Me and the morning glory—a wild
flower some call a weed.
Shades of blue violet magenta
with star shaped centers climbing the
fence row tangled in barbed
wire blooming and dying in a single
day. And you, like them, acquainted
with the night, rose each
day to embrace the light.

At Twilight

In summer,
he performs the evening ritual
stops the tractor in the meadow
to pick a bouquet of wildflowers
purple Ironweed
black-eyed Susan and
field daisies.

Never mind the cows
waiting for their supper.
He gathers the blooms
before pitching the hay,
holds them up in fading light-
flowers for my mother,
his Gracie.

He finds a mason jar
to hold them, fills
it with water from the spigot,
and carries it into the kitchen
where she stands
stirring soup beans on the stove.

He kisses her and sets the jar
on the table—a testimony
at the closing of the day.

Winter Births

The mother cow wasn't due
till late February but went missing
on the coldest of nights in January.
My father found her with twins,
one breathing warmth
into frigid air, the other
stiff like an icicle,
its mother licking the cold body
pausing only to bawl her grief
into the empty pasture.

My father witnessed another
winter birth of twins, his own
son and daughter born on the Solstice,
the difficult birth, my mother's pain,
her sadness in having to let
the aunties take care of the babies
while she regained her strength,
waiting in the long night
for spring to come, in solidarity
with mothers of all creatures.

Hoeing in the Drought

Large, tanned weathered
hands wrap around
the hoe handle
as he chops
morning glory
horse nettle
ragweed
crabgrass.

Dust covers every inch of us, no
rain in the forecast.

He scratches out a lesson in faith:

You've got to believe, he says
in the good times and bad,
you've got to keep
the weeds out
even in the drought
cause if you don't
when it does rain
you wake up
to weeds
tall as trees.

Umbilical Cord

I. When it finally fell from your tiny body,
your grandfather wanted to bury it on the farm
to tie you forever to the hollowed land of your ancestors.
As you grew, he let you steer the tractor over the rich soil,
taught you which plants were weeds in the garden and
marveled at your multiple trips to the wedding buffet.

II. Some of us saw the storm approaching, things falling apart.
So much of this life beyond our control.
We wonder why cords break even when buried in faith.
After his death, I read the will—
He left us a small piece of the land, and
over its scarred surfaces, I signed the disclaimer.

III. The cord still feeds the rose and redbud
and pulls us home in frequent dreams,
where we see the love we planted
ever will remain.

In Which My Parents Are Resurrected

I.

On my birthday,
three months
after my father's death,
I walk in a new neighborhood.
September sun
shines light
on memories of him
in his half-acre
Virginia vegetable garden,
bending over to pluck
green beans and ripening tomatoes.
One summer I carried
a dozen heirlooms
across the country to Seattle
where tomatoes don't have
that same Southern taste.
We turn a corner on our walk
and I see an elderly man
short of stature like my father
in a community garden,
gathering green tomatoes.
I approach, and he asks me
if I like them. I tell him
about frying thick slices
dipped in egg and cornmeal.
My father comes alive in this man
as he fills a bag with the produce
and hands it to me,
a birthday present from heaven.

II.

I've just come from
Black Rock Beach in Maui
where I was consoled
by a giant sea turtle
during a memorial

for my mother.
As I tossed orchid blooms
into the ocean
the turtle swam close
swallowed a petal,
and made eye contact with me.
Her gaze ancient, maternal, assuring
spoke to me: *Your Mother is near.*
An hour later, we stop
at a small church
and see a woman
who looks like my mother.
She says hello, tells us
she is Hawaiian
but has relatives in Virginia
where my mother was born.
And it's her birthday—
she's Aquarian like my mother.
She suggests we pray together,
and holds my hand.
Always remember, she says,
God is everywhere.

III.

My mother died in
May, my father one month
later. I am in the park
running with compacted grief,
crying and praying,
asking God where my parents are.
Seconds after I ask the question,
I hear a woodpecker
as if he is tapping out a response
in the tree above me.
Turns out, there are two of them
and I've never seen woodpeckers
in this park before.
I am reminded

of the many conversations
I had with my father
about the antics of the woodpecker
at the feeder he could see
from his living room chair.
Now miles from that feeder,
and my parents in
another world, they call to me:
Look up, they say
Here we are, together forever.

Scattering the Locks

I. She's humming on the porch swing:

Some glad morning when this life is o'er, I'll Fly Away

> Her hair hangs like a long dark mystery
> waist length, the color of coal.
> She keeps it twisted,
> pinned in a bun
> to the back of her head.
>
> Too hot when hanging down,
> I ask her, why not cut it?
> *Your daddy likes it long*, she says.
> So my mother lives with this length
> for a long time.
>
> She keeps humming:

Just a few more weary days and then, I'll Fly Away

> One steamy summer afternoon
> she sits fanning, sweating,
> asks me to fetch scissors.
>
> I slice thick locks of
> cast iron and they fall
> as crow feathers on wind.
>
> She thinks it odd that I gather them and
> carry the locks west
> to sleep in cities, Seattle, San Francisco.

II. Southern locks lie sleeping
in my cold North drawer,
waiting and knowing
what I could not have known:
How much I would need her locks
 once she was gone.

When the shadows of this life have grown, I'll Fly Away

        She slips into lilac scented spring dawn
        before I can reach her
        I must cross
        The Continental Divide
        Saint Louis,
        Dark hollows, Great Stone Face
        and Elk Knob.

        I call but no one answers the phone:

Like a bird from prisons bars has flown, I'll Fly Away

        She flies and I feel her coming to me
        carried on wings of wonder.

        She arrives and I open the drawer,
        lift the locks, ready myself for release.

I'll Fly Away, Oh Glory, I'll Fly Away
When I die, hallelujah by and by, I'll Fly Away

III.   I don't view the body
            I don't attend the funeral
            I don't receive the ashes,
            I scatter the locks.

            First in the park where I last heard her voice,
            for nesting robins and chickadees
            and in the cemetery near my home.

To a land where joys shall never end, I'll Fly Away

        Next in water:
        Lake Washington, Puget Sound
        Pacific Ocean, and my backyard.

She never traveled far from the family farm,
    or wished to fly on an airplane, preferred train.
    But we never boarded together.
    She never came west,
    only in her dreams.

To a home on God's Celestial Shore, I'll Fly Away

    Now her locks lie scattered around the world:
    Maui Black Rock, Hong Kong and Dark Continent.

    I carry her always with me,
    in locks of hair, DNA,
    cellular memory,
    my own mystery.

Acknowledgments

I am grateful to the editors of the following journals and anthologies where these poems first appeared, sometimes in different versions and with different titles:

The Hollins Critic: "Sleeping with the Serpent"

Entropy: "Scattering the Locks," "Buzzard's Roost"

Still Point Arts Quarterly: "Irish Roots"

The Dead Mule School of Southern Literature: "Bees and Tobacco," "Pocket Knife," "Barn Swing"

Deep South Magazine: "Appalachian Goddess," "Marry Up," "I'm Told How to Get a Pretty Man," "First Grade Teacher"

The Creativity Webzine: "A Bundle of Gladioli," "Day Flowers," "At Twilight"

The Remington Review: "Skirted Soldiers"

Strands Lit Sphere (Strands Publishers): "Miracle in the Chicken Coop Chapel," "What You Can Do," "War Ghosts in the Attic," "He Was Most Afraid of Lightning," "Pearl Harbor"

2020 Waco Cultural Arts Fest WordFest Anthology: "Dominion Over All" (Ball of Fire)

Sage Cigarettes Magazine: "Grapevines"

Pure Slush Anthology, Birth, Lifespan Vol. 1: "Umbilical Cord"

Milk and Cake Press Anthology, Dead of Winter: "Blood Verse"

OpenDoor Magazine: "Blue Ridges"

Tiny Seed Journal: "Cedar Hill" (also selected for "Forest" anthology)

Pine Mountain Sand & Gravel Journal, Volume 24: Appalachian Witness. "Sonnet for the Pit Ponies"

Last Leaves Magazine: "Elephants Remembered," "Keeping the Peace," "Bee Whispering"

The Vincent Brothers Review: "Storytellers," "Civil War Souvenirs," "The Visitation"

"Sleeping with the Serpent" and "Bees and Tobacco" also appear in *The Southern Poetry Anthology, Vol IX: Virginia* (Texas Review Press)

This book is dedicated to my ancestors and storytellers everywhere, especially those whose voices appear in these poems. I am grateful to all the readers and editors who provided valuable feedback, encouragement and support in the making of this book: Sandra Marchetti, Jenny Drai, Erica Wright, David Rigsbee, Annette Sisson, Anna Egan Smucker, Jill McCabe Johnson, Tina Schumann, Roberta Schultz, Michael Wells, Marcia Winston Terry, Jean Kercheval, Leah Maines, Mimi David, Christen Kincaid, and all of the great people at Finishing Line Press, along with my family, friends and many teachers, in particular my First Grade teacher, Mary Rogers at Elk Knob Elementary. Special thanks and much love to my closest and dearest fans: Dave, Ben and Bailey.

Marianne Mersereau is a poet, dancer, mystic, flower lover and tree hugger. She grew up in the forested hills of Appalachia, along Virginia's Crooked Road near the borders of Tennessee, Kentucky and North Carolina. She currently resides among the mist-covered evergreens of Washington State. Marianne is the author of the chapbook *Timbrel* (Finishing Line Press). In the Grip of Grace is her first full-length collection of poetry. Her writing has appeared in *The Hollins Critic, Bella Grace, The Dead Mule School of Southern Literature, Deep South Magazine, Seattle's Poetry on Buses, Remington Review, Fathom Magazine, Entropy, Pine Mountain Sand & Gravel Journal,* and elsewhere, and has been selected for numerous anthologies, including *The Southern Poetry Anthology, Vol. IX: Virginia.* She is a graduate of the University of Virginia at Wise (BA) and Seattle University (MA). She spent a decade teaching elementary school students. Her love of flowers, bees and the natural world earned her the nickname, "Wild Honey." You can follow her on her Facebook page at "Wild Honey Creations."

www.ingramcontent.com/pod-product-compliance
Lightning Source LLC
Chambersburg PA
CBHW020343170426
43200CB00006B/482